**Take Care
of Yourself**

# Caring for Your
# Mental Health

by Mari Schuh

PEBBLE
a capstone imprint

Published by Pebble, an imprint of Capstone.
1710 Roe Crest Drive, North Mankato, Minnesota 56003
capstonepub.com

Library of Congress Cataloging-in-Publication Data is available on the Library of Congress website.
ISBN 9781663976826 (hardcover)
ISBN 9781666326833 (paperback)
ISBN 9781666326840 (ebook pdf)

Summary: Describes how readers can keep their minds healthy through activity, diet, sleep, and stress management.

Image Credits
Capstone Studio: Karon Dubke, 20 (stuffed animals), cover (girl); Getty Images: fotografixx, 10; Shutterstock: Africa Studio, 5, 12, ampcool, cover (tree background), Anna Golant (design element) throughout, ANURAK PONGPATIMET, 7, 15, ESB Professional, 13, fizkes, 9, Lopolo, 11, Monkey Business Images, 19, pixelheadphoto digitalskillet, 16, 17, Prostock-studio, 18, Super Images, 20 (pillow), 21

Editorial Credits
Editor: Erika L. Shores; Designer: Heidi Thompson; Media Researcher: Jo Miller; Production Specialist: Tori Abraham

All internet sites appearing in back matter were available and accurate when this book was sent to press.

# Table of Contents

Words in **bold** are in the glossary.

# What Is Mental Health?

We take care of our bodies every day. It is important to take care of our minds and feelings too.

Mental health is about how we think, feel, and act. It is about how we feel about ourselves and the world around us. Taking care of our minds helps us make good choices. It helps us get along with others.

# Tough Times

People can have tough times. You might be worried about a spelling test. Maybe a friend is moving away. Maybe your dog is sick. Or you are going to a new school.

When life is hard, the way you think, feel, and act might change. You might fight with your friends. You might have trouble sleeping. Having healthy **habits** can help you feel better again.

# Eat Healthy Foods

The food you eat can affect how you think, feel, and act. Yes, it's true! Healthy foods are full of **nutrients**. They keep your energy **steady**. They help you **focus** and feel happy.

Eat many kinds of healthy foods. Choose fruits and vegetables. Whole grains like brown rice are good for you. Eat beans, nuts, and yogurt too. You will feel good!

# Be Active

Get moving! Have fun on a sunny day. Play outside. Ride your bike. Moving your body gives you more energy. It helps you sleep better too. Make it a habit.

Being active is good for your mind in many ways. It helps you feel happy. It also helps you be **confident**. **Stress** is easier to deal with too.

# Friends and Family

People need to spend time alone. But they also need to spend time with others. Being with your friends and family is good for your mind and your health.

Play with your neighbors. Call a friend.
Eat a meal with your family. Put away
devices and toys. Enjoy your food.
Talk with your family at mealtime.

# Take Breaks

Being too busy can make you tired and stressed. Do some of your homework. Then take a break. Rest your body and your mind. Take deep, slow breaths.

Find ways to **relax**. Listen to music. Do **yoga**. Take a warm bath. Paint a picture. Limit your screen time. Be sure to get plenty of sleep every night.

## Good Days and Bad Days

It is OK to have good days and bad days. Everyone does. It is a part of life. Some days you might feel happy. Other days you might be mad or scared. You might worry or cry.

Remember that these feelings are normal.

Everyone is sad or worried sometimes.

Let yourself feel how you really feel.

Feelings change. You can feel better.

# Talk About It

It is healthy to talk about your feelings. When things are not going well, talking about it can make you feel better. Talk when you are ready.

Share your feelings with an adult you trust. You could talk to a **therapist** or **school counselor**. They will listen and help you. This is a good way to be happy and healthy.

# Belly Breathing

Taking deep, slow breaths can help you feel calm and in control. Try this activity to see how breathing can help your mind stay healthy.

## What You Need:

- an area to rest
- a small pillow or a stuffed animal toy

## What You Do:

1. Find a quiet area where you can lie down and rest.
2. Lie down on your back. Then put the pillow or toy on your belly.
3. Take a few deep breaths using your belly. Slowly take in air through your nose. Fill up your belly like a balloon. Slowly let out the air through your mouth.
4. As you breathe, look at the pillow or toy on your belly. Look at it go up and down.
5. Pay attention to your body. How do you feel?

# Glossary

**confident** (KON-fi-duhnt)—sure of yourself

**focus** (FOH-kuss)—to keep your attention on something

**habit** (HAB-it)—something that you do often

**nutrient** (NOO-tree-uhnt)—a part of food, like a vitamin, that is used for growth; nutrients help people stay healthy and strong

**relax** (reh-LAKS)—to calm down

**school counselor** (SKOOL KAUN-suh-luhr)—someone who works in a school and is trained to listen to students, help them with their problems, and give them ideas about what to do

**steady** (STED-ee)—not changing much

**stress** (STRESS)—strain or pressure

**therapist** (THER-uh-pist)—someone who is trained to listen to people, help them with their problems, and give them ideas about what to do

**yoga** (YOH-guh)—exercises and ways of breathing that keep the mind and body healthy

# Read More

Bellisario, Gina. *Shrink Your Stress: How to Keep Calm.* Minneapolis: Lerner Publications, 2021.

Lombardo, Jennifer. *What's Mental Health?* New York: KidHaven Publishing, 2022.

# Internet Sites

*Anxiety—When You Are Worrying About Things* cyh.com/HealthTopics/HealthTopicDetailsKids. aspx?p=335&np=285&id=2224

*Health for Kids!: Feelings* healthforkids.co.uk/feelings

*KidsHealth: Talking About Your Feelings* kidshealth.org/en/kids/talk-feelings.html

# Index

# About the Author

Mari Schuh's love of reading began with cereal boxes at the kitchen table. Today, she is the author of hundreds of nonfiction books for beginning readers. Mari lives in the Midwest with her husband and their sassy house rabbit. Learn more about her at marischuh.com.